Planning for Learning through

ANIMALS

Rachel Sparks Linfield and Christine Warwick
Illustrated by Cathy Hughes

Contents

Published by Step Forward Publishing Limited
25 Cross Street, Leamington Spa, CV32 4PX Tel: 01926 420046 www.practicalpreschool.com
© Step Forward Publishing Limited 2001
Planning for Learning through Animals   ISBN: 1-902438-33-7

MAKING PLANS

WHY PLAN?

The purpose of planning is to make sure that all children enjoy a broad and balanced curriculum. All planning should be useful. Plans are working documents that you spend time preparing, but which should later repay your efforts. Try to be concise. This will help you in finding information quickly when you need it.

LONG-TERM PLANS

Preparing a long-term plan, which maps out the curriculum during a year or even two, will help you to ensure that you are providing a variety of activities and are meeting the statutory requirements of the *Curriculum Guidance for the Foundation Stage* (2000).

Your long-term plan need not be detailed. Divide the time period over which you are planning into fairly equal sections, such as half terms. Choose a topic for each section. Young children benefit from making links between the new ideas they encounter, so as you select each topic, think about the time of year in which you plan to do it. A topic about minibeasts will not be very successful in November!

Although each topic will address all the learning areas, some could focus on a specific area. For example, a topic on Animals would lend itself well to activities relating to Creative Development and Knowledge and Understanding of the World. Another topic might particularly encourage the appreciation of stories. Try to make sure that you provide a variety of topics in your long-term plans.

Autumn 1	Nursery rhymes
Autumn 2	Autumn/Christmas
Spring 1	People who help us
Spring 2	Animals
Summer 1	Clothes
Summer 2	Minibeasts

MEDIUM-TERM PLANS

Medium-term plans will outline the contents of a topic in a little more detail. One way to start this process is by brainstorming on a large piece of paper. Work with your team writing down all the activities you can think of which are relevant to the topic. As you do this it may become clear that some activities go well together. Think about dividing them into themes. The topic of Animals, for example, has themes such as 'Name the animals', 'Where I live', 'Young animals', 'Hide and seek', 'Farm animals' and 'Pets'.

At this stage, it is helpful to make a chart. Write the theme ideas down the side of the chart and put a different area of learning at the top of each column. Now you can insert your brainstormed ideas and will quickly see where there are gaps. As you complete the chart, take account of children's earlier experiences and provide opportunities for them to progress.

Refer back to the *Curriculum Guidance for the Foundation Stage* (2000) and check that you have addressed as many different aspects of it as you can. Once all your medium-term plans are complete, make sure that there are no neglected areas.

DAY-TO-DAY PLANS

The plans you make for each day will outline aspects such as:

- resources needed;

- the way in which you might introduce activities;

- the organisation of adult help;

- size of the group;

- timing;

- key vocabulary.

Identify the learning that each activity is intended to promote. Make a note of any assessments or observations that you are likely to carry out. On your plans, make notes of activities that were particularly successful, or any changes you would make another time.

MAKING PLANS

A FINAL NOTE

Planning should be seen as flexible. Not all groups meet every day, and not all children attend every day. Any part of the plan can be used independently, stretched over a longer period or condensed to meet the needs of any group. You will almost certainly adapt the activities as children respond to them in different ways and bring their own ideas, interests and enthusiasms. The important thing is to ensure that the children are provided with a varied and enjoyable curriculum that meets their individual developing needs.

USING THE BOOK

- Collect or prepare suggested resources as listed on page 21.

- Read the section which outlines links to the Early Learning Goals (pages 4 - 7) and explains the rationale for the topic of Animals.

- For each weekly theme, two activities are described in detail as an example to help you in your planning and preparation. Key vocabulary, questions and learning opportunities are identified.

- The skills chart on page 23 will help you to see at a glance which aspects of children's development are being addressed as a focus each week.

- As children take part in the Animals topic activities, their learning will progress. 'Collecting evidence' on page 22 explains how you might monitor children's achievements.

- Find out on page 20 how the topic can be brought together in a grand finale involving parents, children and friends.

- There is additional material to support the working partnership of families and children in the form of a 'Home links' page, and a photocopiable 'Parent's page' at the back of the book.

It is important to appreciate that the ideas presented in this book will only be a part of your planning. Many activities that will be taking place as routine in your group may not be mentioned. For example, it is assumed that sand, dough, water, puzzles, floor toys and large scale apparatus are part of the ongoing pre-school experience, as are the opportunities which increasing numbers of groups are able to offer for children to develop ICT skills. Role-play areas, stories, rhymes and singing, and group discussion times are similarly assumed to be happening each week although they may not be a focus for described activities.

USING THE EARLY LEARNING GOALS

Having chosen your topic and made your medium-term plans you can use the *Curriculum Guidance for the Foundation Stage* (2000) to highlight the key learning opportunities your activities will address. The Early Learning Goals are split into six areas: Personal, Social and Emotional Development; Communication, Language and Literacy; Mathematical Development; Knowledge and Understanding of the World; Physical Development and Creative Development. Do not expect each of your topics to cover every goal but your long-term plans should allow for all of them to be addressed by the time a child enters Year 1.

The following section highlights parts of the *Curriculum Guidance for the Foundation Stage* in point form to show what children are expected to be able to do by the time they enter Year 1 in each area of learning. These points will be used throughout this book to show how activities for a topic on Animals link to these expectations. For example, Personal, Social and Emotional Development point 7 is 'form good relationships with peers and adults'. Activities suggested which provide the opportunity for children to do this will have the reference PS7. This will enable you to see which parts of the Early Learning Goals are covered in a given week and plan for areas to be revisited and developed.

In addition, you can ensure that activities offer variety in the goals to be encountered. Often a similar activity may be carried out to achieve different learning objectives. For example, during this topic children search for paper ladybirds with numbers on them. Children will be developing mathematical skills as they recognise numbers and count. They will also be using personal and social skills as they talk and collaborate. It is important, therefore, that activities have clearly defined goals so that these may be emphasised during the activity and for recording purposes.

PERSONAL, SOCIAL AND EMOTIONAL DEVELOPMENT (PS)

This area of learning covers important aspects of development that affect the way children learn, behave and relate to others.

By the end of the Foundation Stage, most children will:

PS1   continue to be interested, excited and motivated to learn

PS2   be confident to try activities, initiate ideas and speak in a familiar group

PS3   maintain attention, concentrate and sit quietly when appropriate

PS4   have a developing awareness of their own needs, views and feelings and be sensitive to the needs, views and feelings of others

PS5   have a developing respect for their own cultures and beliefs and those of other people

PS6   respond to significant experiences, showing a range of feelings when appropriate

PS7   form good relationships with peers and adults

PS8   work as a part of a group or class, taking turns and sharing fairly, understanding that there need to be agreed values and codes of behaviour for groups of people, including adults and children, to work together harmoniously

PS9   understand what is right, what is wrong and why

PS10   dress and undress independently and manage their own personal hygiene

PS11   select and use activities and resources independently

PS12   consider the consequences of their words and actions for themselves and others

PS13   understand that people have different needs, views, cultures and beliefs which need to be treated with respect

PS14   understand that they can expect others to treat their needs, views, cultures and beliefs with respect

The topic of Animals offers many opportunities for children's personal, social and emotional development. Time spent discussing how to behave near animals and how to care for pets will encourage children to speak in a group, to be interested and to consider consequences. By playing circle games children will learn to take turns and to understand the need for agreed codes of behaviour. Many of the areas outlined above, though, will be covered on an almost incidental basis as children carry out the activities described in this book for the other areas of children's learning. During undirected free choice times they will be developing PS11 whilst any small group activity that involves working with an adult will help children to work towards PS7.

COMMUNICATION, LANGUAGE AND LITERACY (L)

The objectives set out in the *National Literacy Strategy: Framework for Teaching* for the reception year are in line with these goals. By the end of the Foundation Stage, most children will be able to:

L1   enjoy listening to and using spoken and written language and readily turn to it in their play and learning

L2   explore and experiment with sounds, words and texts

L3   listen with enjoyment and respond to stories, songs and other music, rhymes and poems and make up their own stories, songs, rhymes and poems

L4   use language to imagine and recreate roles and experiences

L5   use talk to organise, sequence and clarify thinking, ideas, feelings and events

L6   sustain attentive listening, responding to what they have heard by relevant comments, questions or actions;

L7   interact with others, negotiating plans and activities and taking turns in conversation

L8   extend their vocabulary, exploring the meaning and sounds of new words

L9   retell narratives in the correct sequence, drawing on the language patterns of stories

L10   speak clearly and audibly with confidence and control and show awareness of the listener, for example by their use of conventions such as greetings, 'please' and 'thank you'

L11   hear and say initial and final sounds in words and short vowel sounds within words

L12   link sounds to letters, naming and sounding letters of the alphabet

L13   read a range of familiar and common words and simple sentences independently

L14   show an understanding of the elements of stories such as main character, sequence of events, and openings and how information can be found in non-fiction texts to answer questions about where, who, why and how

L15   know that print carries meaning and, in English, is read from left to right and top to bottom

L16   attempt writing for various purposes, using features of different forms such as lists, stories and instructions

L17   write their own names and other things such as labels and captions, and begin to form sentences, sometimes using punctuation

L18   use their phonic knowledge to write simple regular words and make phonetically plausible attempts at more complex words

L19   use a pencil and hold it effectively to form recognisable letters, most of which are correctly formed

There is a wide range of quality fiction and non-fiction books which feature animals. A number of the activities suggested for the theme of Animals are based on well-known picture books and stories. They allow children to enjoy listening to the books and to respond in a variety of ways to what they hear, reinforcing and extending their vocabularies. Throughout the topic, opportunities are described in which children are encouraged to use descriptive vocabulary and to see some of their ideas recorded in both pictures and words. Role-play areas are described that will allow children to use their imaginations as they wander through a jungle and visit a pet shop.

MATHEMATICAL DEVELOPMENT (M)

The key objectives in the *National Numeracy Strategy: Framework for Teaching* for the reception year are in line with these goals. By the end of the Foundation Stage, most children should be able to:

M1   say and use number names in order in familiar contexts

M2   count reliably up to ten everyday objects

M3   recognise numerals 1 to 9

M4   use language such as 'more' or 'less' to compare two numbers

M5   in practical activities and discussion begin to use the vocabulary involved in adding and subtracting

M6   find one more or one less than a number from one to ten.

M7   begin to relate addition to combining two groups of objects and subtraction to 'taking away'

M8   talk about, recognise and recreate simple patterns

M9   use language such as 'circle' or 'bigger' to describe the shape and size of solids and flat shapes

M10   use everyday words to describe position

M11   use developing mathematical ideas and methods to solve practical problems

M12   use language such as 'greater', 'smaller', 'heavier' or 'lighter' to compare quantities

The theme of Animals provides a meaningful context for mathematical activities. Children are given the opportunity to count a wide variety of animals, legs and markings and to begin to develop language for addition and subtraction. There are opportunities for children to explore size as they compare animals. A number of counting rhymes with actions and games that use simple equipment are suggested to reinforce the theme.

KNOWLEDGE AND UNDERSTANDING OF THE WORLD (K)

By the end of the Foundation Stage, most children will be able to:

K1   investigate objects and materials by using all of their senses as appropriate

K2   find out about, and identify, some features of living things, objects and events they observe

K3   look closely at similarities, differences, patterns and change

K4   ask questions about why things happen and how things work

K5   build and construct with a wide range of objects, selecting appropriate resources and adapting their work where necessary

K6   select tools and techniques they need to shape, assemble and join materials they are using

K7   find out about and identify the uses of everyday technology and use information and communication technology and programmable toys to support their learning

K8   find out about past and present events in their own lives, and in those of their families and other people they know

K9   observe, find out about and identify features in the place they live and the natural world

K10   begin to know about their own cultures and beliefs and those of other people

K11   find out about their environment and talk about those features they like and dislike

The topic of Animals offers opportunities for children to make observations, to ask questions and to compare. They can observe a range of animal markings and colours and investigate camouflage. By looking at pictures of wild animals they will gain an understanding of features that help them to be suited to particular habitats. Activities such as making ponds and honey biscuits will help children to gain a greater understanding of the properties of materials.

PHYSICAL DEVELOPMENT (PD)

By the end of the Foundation Stage, most children will be able to:

PD1   move with confidence, imagination and in safety

PD2   move with control and coordination

PD3   show awareness of space, of themselves and of others

PD4   recognise the importance of keeping healthy and those things which contribute to this

PD5   recognise the changes that happen to their bodies when they are active

PD6   use a range of small and large equipment

PD7   travel around, under, over and through balancing and climbing equipment

PD8   handle tools, objects, construction and malleable materials safely and with increasing control

Activities such as playing with playdough and construction toys will offer experience of PD8. Through pretending to be animals in a variety of places and situations children will have the opportunity to move with control and imagination and develop awareness of safety and space. Through using a range of small and large equipment as they build animal homes and walk on spirals they will be encouraged to develop their coordination and control.

CREATIVE DEVELOPMENT (C)

By the end of the Foundation Stage, most children will be able to:

C1   explore colour, texture, shape, form and space in two or three dimensions

C2   recognise and explore how sounds can be changed, sing simple songs from memory, recognise repeated sounds and sound patterns and match movements to music

C3   respond in a variety of ways to what they see, hear, smell, touch and feel

C4   use their imagination in art and design, music, dance, imaginative and role play and stories

C5   express and communicate their ideas, thoughts and feelings by using a widening range of materials, suitable tools, imaginative and role play, movement, designing and making, and a variety of songs and musical instruments

During this topic children will experience working with a variety of materials as they make animal collages, print with sponges, weave and finger paint. They will be able to develop their skills of painting and colour mixing as they paint animals and patterns and work towards C1. A number of songs that involve animals have been suggested which could have actions and percussion added to allow children to use their imagination in music. Throughout all the activities children are encouraged to talk about what they see and feel as they communicate their ideas in painting, music, collage work and role play.

WEEK 1

NAME THE ANIMALS

PERSONAL, SOCIAL AND EMOTIONAL DEVELOPMENT

- During a circle time show children a variety of pictures of animals. Collaboratively sort the pictures into ones which children might have as pets and ones that are found in the wild. (PS3)

- Read *Dinner Time* by Jan Pienkowski (Orchard Books). Ask children to say the names of the animals in the book. Where do children think that the animals might live? How do children think they would feel if they were an animal meeting a human for the first time? Discuss the importance of being quiet and gentle near animals. (PS9, 12)

COMMUNICATION, LANGUAGE AND LITERACY

- Use *Dear Zoo* by Rod Campbell (Puffin) as the stimulus for making lift-the-flap concertina books (see activity opposite). (L3, 11, 19)

- Enjoy using the jungle role-play area (see 'Display'). (L1)

- Start an animal alphabet that can be added to as the topic progresses. On large sheets of card write each letter of the alphabet in lower case. Invite children to suggest animals that begin with each letter and to draw a picture or write the word of their choice. (L12, 16)

MATHEMATICAL DEVELOPMENT

- Use pictures and mathematical language to make sentences to describe animals (see activity opposite). (M12)

- Sort pictures or toy animals into hoops according to features such as number of legs, has a beak and so on. Ask children to count how many animals there are in each hoop. (M2)

KNOWLEDGE AND UNDERSTANDING OF THE WORLD

- Introduce the book *Rumble in the Jungle* by Giles Andreae (Orchard Books). Encourage children to identify the animals and to describe where they are hiding. Use the pictures to learn about the names of animal body parts. (K2)

- Provide each child with a picture of an animal (animal snap cards are ideal). Encourage children to describe their animals and to notice similarities and differences between animals. (K3)

PHYSICAL DEVELOPMENT

- Play a game in which children are walking stealthily through a jungle. Help the children to imagine they are looking through binoculars to find hiding animals. Whenever the 'lion' roars the children have to freeze. (PD1, 2, 3)

- Encourage children to pretend to move as if they are a chosen animal. (PD1, 2, 3)

- Enjoy making a jungle of animals with playdough and animal-shaped cutters. (PD8)

CREATIVE DEVELOPMENT

- Using *Rumble in the Jungle* by Giles Andreae (Orchard Books), talk about the sounds that each animal makes. Encourage children to join in with the sounds. Invite children to take it in turn to play 'I spy an animal that sounds like this.' (C2)

- Look at pictures that show animal patterns such as the stripes of a zebra or the spots of a leopard. Provide each child with a large pre-drawn picture of a tiger, zebra, snake, leopard, cheetah, jaguar or giraffe. Use sponges, rollers and ready-mixed paint to produce the animal's pattern. (C1)

is taller than

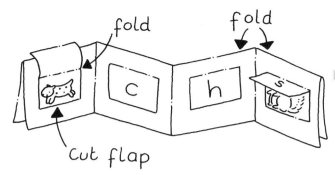

fold   fold

Cut flap

ACTIVITY: MAKING 'DEAR ZOO' FLAP BOOKS

Learning opportunity: Responding to a story, recognising initial sounds and making books.

Early Learning Goal: Communication, Language and Literacy. Children will be able to listen with enjoyment and respond to stories, and make up their own stories. They will hear and say initial sounds in words. They will use a pencil and hold it effectively to form recognisable letters.

Resources: *Dear Zoo* by Rod Campbell (Puffin); pencils; crayons; for each child a flap book made from A3 sized stiff paper (see diagram).

Key vocabulary: Names of animals, flap book, page, cover, author.

Organisation: Whole group introduction, small group practical activity.

WHAT TO DO:

Show the group *Dear Zoo* by Rod Campbell. Point out where the author's name is and explain that he wrote the book. As you read, encourage the children to join in with the repeated phrases and predict what might be under each flap. Show the group the prepared flap books. Explain that they are each going to make their own 'Dear Zoo' book. Encourage them to think of the animals that they might like to put under each flap and of the one that they would keep.

Working with children in small groups, help them to draw the pictures of the animals and to write the initial letter of each one on the flaps. Decorate the covers and help children to write their names on them. When all the books have been completed, encourage children to 'read' theirs to the group and to enjoy guessing which animal might be under a friend's flap,

ACTIVITY: MAKING ANIMAL SENTENCES

Learning opportunity: Using language to describe size.

Early Learning Goal: Mathematical Development. Children will be able to use language such as 'greater', 'smaller', 'heavier' or 'lighter' to compare quantities.

Resources: Pictures of an elephant, a giraffe, a zebra, a snake, an ant, a worm and a butterfly. (The pictures must show the relative sizes of the animals to allow children to compare them.) Strips of card showing the following phrases: 'is smaller than', 'is greater than', 'is taller than', 'is shorter than', 'is heavier than', 'is lighter than'. Sticky Velcro or magnetic tape.

Key vocabulary: Names of animals, smaller, greater, taller, shorter, heavier, lighter.

Organisation: Small group.

WHAT TO DO:

Show the group the pictures of the animals. Describe one of the animals using phrases from the key vocabulary list, for example: 'This animal is very tall. It is taller than ....' Ask children to point to the animal that they think you are describing. Depending upon how confident the children are in using the language invite one to describe an animal for the group to pick out. Introduce the phrase card 'is taller than'. Place the picture of the giraffe at the start of the phrase and ask for suggestions of which animals could finish it. On future occasions encourage children to make their own sentences.

DISPLAY

Create a jungle area to use for role play. Cover a large board at floor level with a variety of green backing papers. Cut out and stick on 3-d leaves, grasses and trees. Place cushions covered with animal prints or green fabric on the floor along with a safe, real plant in a plastic pot and a green box with the animal books used during the week. Display the printed animals with name labels among the leaves and encourage children to visit their jungle.

 is shorter than

WEEK 2
WHERE I LIVE

PERSONAL, SOCIAL AND EMOTIONAL DEVELOPMENT

- During a circle time talk about the homes that children live in. What is special about the home? Look at pictures of a variety of homes and ask children which ones they would like to live in and why. (PS2, 14)

- Show the children a selection of animal homes such as a bird box, a bat box, shells and honeycomb and pictures of ones such as a wasp's nest and a bird's nest. Encourage the children to think about which animal might live in each and to give reasons for their suggestions. (PS2, 3)

COMMUNICATION, LANGUAGE AND LITERACY

- Use the big book form of *Over in the Grasslands* by Anna Wilson and Alison Bartlett (Macmillan Children's Books) to help children to identify animals that live in grasslands. Encourage them to enjoy listening to and joining in with the rhymes. (L3)

- Read *Larry Lion's Rumbling Rhymes* by Giles Andreae and David Wojtowycz (Macmillan's Children's Books), encouraging children to join in the rhymes. Help children to recognise pairs of words with identical initial sounds such as Larry Lion. Make a collection of animal names using children's names, such as Alice Alligator, Barnabas Bat and Chen Chicken. (L3, 11)

MATHEMATICAL DEVELOPMENT

- Give each child a wicker basket or a drawing of a nest. Play a game in which children take it in turns to shake a die and collect the corresponding number of eggs cut from card. The aim is to collect exactly ten in each nest or basket. (M2, 7)

- Repeat the nest game but this time each child starts with ten eggs and then 'hatches' the eggs when the die is thrown. After each throw, encourage children to say how many eggs they had, how many have hatched and the number that remain. (M2, 5)

- Enjoy reciting the action number rhyme 'Birds in the Birdcage' by Carolyn Graham in *First Verses* (Oxford University Press). (M1)

KNOWLEDGE AND UNDERSTANDING OF THE WORLD

- Provide a selection of toy animals and pictures of animal homes. Ask the children to place the animals in their homes. Introduce children to the names for animal homes such as nest, badger's sett and squirrel's drey. (K9)

- Show children a picture or a piece of honeycomb. Explain that honeycomb is a home for bees. Encourage children to notice the hexagonal structure and the holes for bees to go into. Provide each child with a card hexagon on which to draw a bee. When all the hexagons are complete, put them together to make a large group honeycomb (see 'Display'). (K2)

PHYSICAL DEVELOPMENT

- Use hoops, a tunnel, mats and cushions to play the 'Animals go home!' movement game (see activity opposite). (PD1, 3, 7)

- Help children to imagine that they are animals that have to build homes. Encourage them to think about the size of the animal that they choose to be and the size and weight of the materials that the animal uses for building the home. Set out a selection of boxes, bean bags, toy bricks and so on for the animals to collect, one piece at a time in a busy manner and to build their nest/home. Before the session finishes invite children to talk about their animal home and to explain why it is special. (PD1, 8)

CREATIVE DEVELOPMENT

- Make pom-pom bees (see activity opposite). (C1)

- Provide each child with an outline of a habitat such as a jungle, mountains or a meadow. Put out a selection of small pieces of a variety of textures and colours of materials for children to use to make collages. Encourage them to think about the colours they choose and how to stick materials to create sky, land and plant effects. (C1)

- Encourage children to look closely at the habitat collage they have made and to describe an animal that might like to live in it. Invite children to select an animal shape cut from card, to colour it by printing with sponges and ready-mixed paint and, when dry, to stick it on to the habitat. (C1)

ACTIVITY: 'ANIMALS GO HOME!' GAME

Learning opportunity: Moving imaginatively to music.

Early Learning Goal: Physical Development. Children will be able to move with confidence, imagination and in safety. They will show awareness of space, of themselves and of others. They will travel around, under, over and through balancing and climbing equipment.

Resources: A circuit of climbing and balancing equipment, a tunnel, hoops and mats; a tape or CD of *The Carnival of Animals* by Saint-Saens or similar music with an animal theme.

Key vocabulary: This will depend on the names of animals children choose to be and the words that describe how these animals move.

Organisation: Whole group.

WHAT TO DO:

Sitting in a circle on the floor ask children to close their eyes and to listen to an extract from *The Carnival of Animals*. Tell the group the title of the music and ask them to tell you the names of the animals that they can 'see' in their minds. Where do they think the animals are? What are they doing? Invite individual children to show the group how they think the animals are moving.

Show the group the circuit of equipment that has been set out. Introduce them to animal homes such as a cave for bears (climbing frame); a swamp and an island (mats); a log (bench) and so on. Ask the children to stand around the circuit and to move as animals to the music. When the music stops they must move to the nearest home and be an animal that might live there. Encourage children to listen carefully to the music and to be aware of and use all the available space.

ACTIVITY: MAKING POM-POM BEES

Learning opportunity: Using a variety of materials and working collaboratively.

Early Learning Goal: Creative Development. Children will be able to explore colour, texture, shape, form and space in two or three dimensions.

Resources: Thick wool in black and a variety of shades of yellow; blue tissue paper, cellophane or net; glue; scissors; black and white card; a ready made pom-pom bee; for each child two thick card circles of diameter about 7 cm with a circle of 3-4 cm removed from the centre.

Key vocabulary: Wind, bee, wing, eye, tie, black, yellow, white.

Organisation: Small group.

WHAT TO DO:

Show children a picture of bees near a honeycomb. Explain that they are going to make a pom-pom bee to hang from the ceiling in front of the honeycomb that the group has already made. Give each child two card circles and show them how to wind wool tightly around the two circles with a layer of black wool, then yellow and then more black until the central hole has almost been filled. When finished, show children how to cut the wool at the outer edge.

Tie two long pieces of strong wool firmly around the centre with several knots. Carefully remove the card circles (which can be kept for re-use) and fluff the pom-pom, trimming odd ends. Cut wings from blue paper or fabric and attach these by tying firmly with one of the long lengths of wool at the centre of the pom-pom. Hold the other wool length to see how the bee hangs and then invite children to cut and stick on eyes to their bee. Use a permanent pen to write each child's initials on their bee's wing and hang them near the card honeycomb.

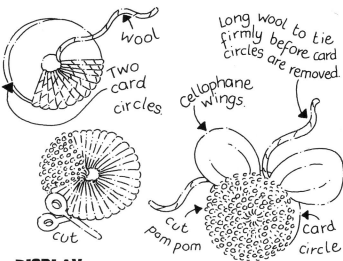

DISPLAY

Mount the card hexagons on black card or sugar paper and trim to give a border of 1 cm. Involve children in arranging them together as a tessellating honeycomb background. Hang the pom-pom bees in front at varying heights. Display the habitat collages on a board with a table in front. On the table put out a selection of toy animals and non-fiction animal picture books. Encourage children to place the toys near the habitats that they might wish to live in and to use the books to find other animals that would also be at home there.

WEEK 3
HIDE AND SEEK

PERSONAL, SOCIAL AND EMOTIONAL DEVELOPMENT

- During a circle time introduce the week's theme. Hide five soft toy animals around the room where they can be seen from the circle but not immediately visible. Talk about why animals hide and how it might feel to be found. As a group, find the animals. (PS7, 8)

- Play 'Hide and seek'. Before playing, talk about the rules for the game so that children understand where they may hide, who will do the seeking and the signal for coming out if people are not found. Help children to understand why the game has rules. Afterwards, talk about how it felt to hide, to seek and to be caught. (PS8, 9)

COMMUNICATION, LANGUAGE AND LITERACY

- Use cardboard boxes to make an interactive display of soft toy animals. Help children to write a caption for their toy to explain what it is. Stick the caption on a flap for a door. Invite children to look at the captions and enjoy guessing who is inside. (L1, 17)

- Read *The Mixed-Up Chameleon* by Eric Carle (Picture Puffin). Discuss why the chameleon changed colour at the start of the book and why some animals are camouflaged. Encourage children to look closely at the pictures and to identify the creatures. (L3, 5)

MATHEMATICAL DEVELOPMENT

- Use the interactive display of toy animals as data to make a bar chart or pictogram. Encourage children to think about how the animals should be grouped, to count the number in each group and to record the number of animals in each set with pictures. (M1, 2, 4)

- Use the hiding snails counting rhyme (see activity opposite). (M1, 2)

KNOWLEDGE AND UNDERSTANDING OF THE WORLD

- Show children pictures of animals that have brightly coloured patterns. Explain that the colours warn other creatures to stay away. Talk about colours that are used in the human world for warnings. Provide each child with a template of a ladybird to be coloured with warning colours and patterns. (K1, 2)

- Tell children the Aboriginal creation myth about the snake. Show illustrations from a book about the snake such as *Kum-Man-Gur The Rainbow Servant* by James Cowan (Barefoot Books) or *Dream Time Aboriginal Stories* by Oodgero (Lothrop, Lee & Shepard Books). Use brightly coloured paper, sequins and shiny paper to make rainbow snakes. (K1, 2)

PHYSICAL DEVELOPMENT

- Play a version of musical statues in which children are animals walking through a jungle. When the music stops, the animals freeze so that they cannot be seen by predators. (PD1, 2, 3)

- Chalk large spiral shells on the playground. Encourage children to practise walking with bean bags on their heads, following the spiral lines as they journey to hide inside the shells. (PD1, 2)

CREATIVE DEVELOPMENT

- Use *The Mixed-Up Chameleon* by Eric Carle (Picture Puffin) as the stimulus for making mixed-up animal pictures (see activity opposite). (C4)

- Look at pictures that show a variety of animals with clear markings such as leopard spots and zebra stripes. Cover A2 sized pieces of paper with animal patterns. Then, using materials in the same colours as the A2 paintings, make A4-sized collages or woven patches. (C1)

ACTIVITY: USING THE SNAIL FINGER RHYME

Learning opportunity: Using a number rhyme to encourage counting backwards from ten.

Early Learning Goal: Mathematical Development. Children will be able to say and use number names in order in familiar contexts. They will count reliably up to ten everyday objects.

Resources: Picture of a snail.

Key vocabulary: Snail, shell, numbers one to ten, 'How many?'.

Organisation: Whole group.

WHAT TO DO:

Show children a picture of a snail. Help them to notice the shell and to think of the times when it might be useful. Explain that the shell is particularly useful when the snail wants to hide away.

Recite the number rhyme below, starting with five snails. Encourage children to join in with the words as well as the actions and gradually increase the number of snails at the start. This activity can also be extended by varying the number of snails that fall asleep.

Ten snails slither slowly	*Show ten fingers*
Leaving silver trails	*Use arm to slither on other arm*
But when it rains and thunders	*Clap on 'thunders'*
Inside go the snails!	*Hide head under arms*
The sun comes out	*Move open hands in circles*
But one snail's fast asleep	*Mime being asleep*
And only nine snails	*Show nine fingers*
Come out their shells to peep!	*Use arm to slither on other arm*

ACTIVITY: MAKING MIXED-UP ANIMALS

Learning opportunity: Drawing, colouring and collaborating to make mixed-up animals.

Early Learning Goal: Creative Development. Children will be able to use their imagination in art and design.

Resources: A4-sized white cartridge paper or card divided into three equal 10-cm pieces; pencils; felt pens; either a spiral binder or a laminator.

Key vocabulary: Head, body, legs, names of animals.

Organisation: Small group.

WHAT TO DO:

Give each child a piece of A4 white cartridge paper or card. Point out the three sections and ask them to draw a head of an animal in the first. Encourage them to make the head as large as possible and to draw between two pencil dots so that all the heads are about the same width. Then ask them to draw the body and the legs, again using dots to maintain the widths of the body parts. Once completed the animals can be used in a variety of ways.

Collaborative picture:
The animals are cut into three. Each child retains their head piece and is then given pieces from two other children. The pieces are glued together, cut out and mounted on black sugar paper. The mixed-up animals can be given imaginary names and hidden in the jungle made in Week 1.

Flip books:
The group's pictures can be spiral bound before being cut. When cut, children will enjoy seeing their artwork in a range of different animals.

Game:
If the pictures are laminated before being cut they can be used to make a variety of animals and to play pelmanism.

DISPLAY

Display the paintings of animal patterns on a noticeboard with their corresponding collages/woven patches at the centre. Encourage children to walk away from the displays and to notice when it becomes difficult to spot the collages/patches.

On a table, put out all the animal books used during the week along with the mixed-up animal flip books. Add the rainbow snakes to the jungle made in Week 1. Hide the patterned ladybirds around the room and invite children to seek them out. Encourage them to notice which patterns act as a camouflage and which help the insects to be clearly visible.

WEEK 4
YOUNG ANIMALS

PERSONAL, SOCIAL AND EMOTIONAL DEVELOPMENT

- Tell or read the story of 'Milly-Molly-Mandy Minds a Baby' from *Further Doings of Milly-Molly-Mandy* by Joyce Lankester Brisley (Puffin). Talk about the way Milly-Molly-Mandy took care of the hedgehog. (PS3, 4)

- During a circle time show children a variety of pictures of animals and their young. Include pictures of people as well. Discuss what the babies need to keep them safe and happy. (PS3, 4)

COMMUNICATION, LANGUAGE AND LITERACY

- Enjoy sharing a book that depicts animals and their young such as *I Don't Want to Go to Bed!* or *Little Tiger's Big Surprise!* by Julie Sykes and Tim Warnes (Little Tiger Press, Magi Publications); *Can't You Sleep Little Bear?* or *Let's Go Home Little Bear* by Martin Waddell (Walker Books); *Just You and Me* by Sam McBratney (Walker Books) and *Peace at Last* by Jill Murphy (Walker Books). Help children to notice how the young animals were looked after by their parents. Make a display of the books and encourage children to retell the tales using the picture cues. (L3, 9)

- From card make jig-saw labels which include the name of an animal and pictures of the adult and its young (see diagram). Give each child a jig-saw piece and tell a story about all the animals. When the animal's name is mentioned the children stand up and make the jig-saw. (L13)

MATHEMATICAL DEVELOPMENT

- Put out a selection of plastic animals. Ask children to sort the animals into adults and young and to count the number in each set. Sort the animals into adults with their young. Which animal has the most young? Is there an animal without young? Encourage children to use the correct names for the young animals such as cub, lamb and calf. (M1, 2, 4)

- Make a Noah's ark counting book (see activity opposite). (M1)

KNOWLEDGE AND UNDERSTANDING OF THE WORLD

- Use *The Very Hungry Caterpillar* by Eric Carle (Puffin Books) or *Who Am I?* by Judith Nicholls (Ladybird) as the stimulus for making life-cycle wheels (see activity opposite). (K2, 3)

- Make a collection of non-fiction picture books and pictures to show the life-cycles of a variety of insects and other animals. Help children to realise that the changes that happen are gradual and take place over time. Encourage them to compare the pictures of real animals with the illustrations in fiction books. (K2, 3)

PHYSICAL DEVELOPMENT

- Encourage children to move in pairs as an adult animal with its young. Encourage the young animals to mirror what their parents do. (PD1, 2, 3)

- Use self-hardening malleable materials to depict the life-cycle of a butterfly. When the models have dried, encourage children to paint them. Display the models by sticking them with double-sided sticky tape onto leaves cut from card. (PD8)

CREATIVE DEVELOPMENT

- Make a group display of a mother with young hedgehogs. Help children to draw around their hands and to cut them out of black, grey and brown sugar papers. Show children how to stick their hands on pre-drawn hedgehogs so that the fingers are loose and overlap to make spiky hedgehogs. (C1)

- Use salt dough and animal cutters to make mother and young animal pairs. Put a hole through each animal. When dry, hang the animals up along with name labels to make a group mobile. (C1)

ACTIVITY: MAKING NOAH'S ARK COUNTING BOOKS

Learning opportunity: Making individual books for counting activities.

Early Learning Goal: Mathematical Development. Children will be able to say and use number names in order in familiar contexts.

Resources: Crayons, pencils; a picture book of the Noah's ark tale such as *Noah's Ark* by Lucy Cousins (Walker Books); animal templates of adult and young animals; small pieces of card; for each child a card ark with an envelope stuck inside (see diagram).

Key vocabulary: Names of animals, numbers to ten, how many?, ark, pair, adult, young.

Organisation: Small group.

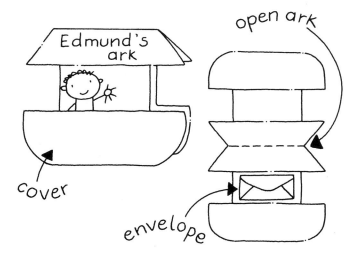

WHAT TO DO:

Use the picture book of Noah's ark to remind children what the ark was. Count the animals on each page and check children know what the word 'pair' means. Show children the arks made from card and explain that they are each going to have one. Help children to write on the roof their name to give the title _____'s Ark and to draw a picture of themselves on the ark. Ask children which animals they would like to put in their arks. Encourage children to draw the animals on separate pieces of card along with young animals. When each pair of animals has been completed, show children how to place them inside the envelope in their ark. Use the books for counting practice. Help children to compare the number of animals in each ark.

ACTIVITY: LIFE-CYCLE WHEELS

Learning opportunity: Recognising and illustrating stages in animal life-cycles.

Early Learning Goal: Knowledge and Understanding of the World. Children will be able to find out and identify some features of living things. They will look closely at change.

Resources: For each child two large circles cut from A4 white card, one with almost a quarter cut away; crayons, pencils; a split pin; pictures to show the butterfly life-cycle; *The Very Hungry Caterpillar* by Eric Carle (Puffin Books); a completed life-cycle dial.

Key vocabulary: Egg, chrysalis, caterpillar, butterfly, hatch, leaf, leaves, life-cycle dial.

Organisation: Small group.

WHAT TO DO:

Look at the pictures in *The Very Hungry Caterpillar*. Help children to identify the eggs, caterpillar, chrysalis and butterfly. Talk about the foods that the caterpillar in the book ate and what a real one might prefer. Show children a completed life-cycle dial and ask them to say what each picture shows.

Provide each child with a card circle divided into four sections by a pencil line. Ask them to draw an egg on a leaf in one section, a caterpillar in the next one, and so on. When each stage of the cycle has been drawn, encourage the children to colour the pictures in realistic colours. Finally, show them how to attach the circle with a quarter removed to their circle with a split pin to complete their life-cycle dial.

DISPLAY

Cover a large noticeboard with autumnal colours and display the hand-print hedgehogs. On a table, set out the models depicting the life-cycle of a butterfly. On a nearby board that is at child height, put up the life-cycle dials. Encourage children to use the dials and to take care when turning them.

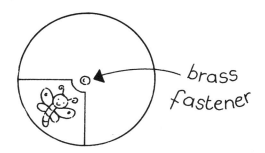

WEEK 5
FARM ANIMALS

PERSONAL, SOCIAL AND EMOTIONAL DEVELOPMENT

- Show children some milk, hard-boiled eggs and wool and pictures of sheep, dairy cows and hens. Talk about farmers, farms and the way we are helped by their produce. Help children to identify where milk, eggs and wool come from. (If a child in the group is allergic to eggs or milk, pictures should be used.) (PS1, 4)

- Invite someone who keeps sheep for wool, cows for milk or hens for eggs to come and talk about looking after animals. Talk about the importance of treating animals with care and the need to wash hands after being near animals. (PS1, 7)

COMMUNICATION, LANGUAGE AND LITERACY

- Make animal family cards that have a picture of the animal on one side and its name on the other. Sort the cards into family sets by pictures and words. Play a game in which children pick animals according to clues such as 'Find two animals that rhyme' (lamb, ram). Clues could also be based on initial and final sounds. (L11, 12, 13)

- Use 'Little Bo Peep' as the stimulus for rhyming work with children's names. Ask children to suggest things which they might have lost such as 'Little Sue has lost the glue'. Where a rhyme cannot be found ask children to suggest something that begins with the same letter. (L3, 11, 13)

MATHEMATICAL DEVELOPMENT

- Decorate a box with a lid as a farm building. Ask children to count as you place five animals in the box. Put on the lid and ask how many animals there are in the box. Open the box, take out one animal and replace the lid. Ask children how many animals are in the box now. Repeat the activity several times encouraging children to picture the animals in the box and to use the language of addition and subtraction. When children are confident, encourage them to close their eyes and to see the box in their minds. (M2, 5)

- Give each child a strip with up to five farm animals without legs drawn on it. Check that children know what the animals are, how many legs each one should have and then ask them to draw the legs. Ask the children to count how many animals they each have. Who has the most? Who has the fewest animals? Which strip do they think will have the most legs? Will any strips have the same number? Count and compare. (M1, 2, 4)

KNOWLEDGE AND UNDERSTANDING OF THE WORLD

- Read *Honey Biscuits* by Meredith Hooper (Kingfisher). Use the illustrations to make a list of all the animals that were necessary to produce the ingredients for the biscuits. Use the recipe at the end of the book to make honey biscuits. (K1)

- Read a story about sheep such as *Morag and the Lamb* by Joan Lingard (Walker Books); *Emma's Lamb* by Kim Lewis (Walker Books) or *Friska the Sheep that was too Small* by Rob Lewis. Look at the illustrations and notice the sheep's fleeces. Make a group display of items made from wool. (K1)

PHYSICAL DEVELOPMENT

- Use the song 'Old Macdonald had a farm' for an animal follow-my-leader game. When the animals are mentioned the leader pretends to be the animal and everyone else copies. The leader then goes to the back of the line, leaving a new leader for a new verse. (PD1, 2, 3)

- Make sheep from clay (see activity opposite). (PD8)

CREATIVE DEVELOPMENT

- Make farm animal finger puppets (see activity opposite). (C1)

- Enjoy acting out and providing percussion for the story of the 'Little Red Hen' as outlined in *Three Singing Pigs: Making music with traditional stories* by Kaye Umansky (A & C Black)

ACTIVITY: MAKING CLAY SHEEP

Learning opportunity: Using clay and talking about the way it behaves.

Early Learning Goal: Physical Development. Children will be able to handle tools, objects, construction and malleable materials safely and with increasing control.

Resources: Sheep pictures, toys and ornaments that have woolly fleece; soft, white clay; white and black ready-mixed paint; large-holed sieves.

Key vocabulary: Sheep, lamb, fleece, woolly, sieve, clay, hole, push.

Organisation: Small group.

WHAT TO DO:

Show children the pictures/toys of sheep. Explain that they are each going to make a sheep from clay. First, give children the opportunity to handle the clay. Encourage them to roll a small piece between their hands to form a ball. Roll the ball on the table top with the palm of one hand to form a fat sausage and then between the fingers of both hands to form a long thin worm. Roll it back into a ball.

To make the sheep, divide the ball into six pieces to be used as the head, body and legs. Roll out the four smaller pieces for legs. Show children how to make body and head shapes and how to attach the legs by gently squashing the joints together.

Finally, force a small ball of clay through a sieve using a thumb. The clay will be extruded like thin strands of wool. Lay the strands over the sheep's body and tap gently to secure. Use a pencil to press into the clay to give markings for eyes and a mouth.

The clay will harden if left on a sunny window sill. Once dry, it can be painted.

ACTIVITY: FARM ANIMAL FINGER PUPPETS

Learning opportunity: Making felt puppets for collaborative play.

Early Learning Goal: Creative Development. Children will be able to explore colour, texture, shape, form and space in two or three dimensions.

Resources: Pictures of farm animals; examples of finger puppets; for each child a plastic large-eyed needle; two felt pieces large enough to go over two fingers with needle holes punched out (see diagram); felt pieces to decorate the puppets; glue; stiff plastic

(cut from plastic cartons) to insert inside the puppets when gluing on the decoration.

Key vocabulary: Finger puppet, names of animals and colours, needle, felt, wool.

Organisation: Whole group introduction followed by practical activity for pairs of children.

WHAT TO DO:

For the whole group introduction show the children the completed finger puppets. Explain that during the week they will each make a finger puppet of a farm animal. Ask for suggestions of animals that might be made. Encourage children to think about the colours of felt that they will need and how they could make their puppet look like their chosen animal. Make a list of the children's names and the animals that they wish to make. Some children may like to gain ideas from books and pictures.

Later in the week, work with pairs of children to sew the bodies. Show them how to oversew with wool through the prepared needle holes. Use a permanent felt pen to write the child's initials inside the bottom of the puppet. When all bodies have been sewn, invite pairs of children who are making similar animals to come and stick pieces of felt onto their animal bodies. Show them how to insert a piece of plastic inside their puppet so that glue will not seep through. Once dry, encourage children to use them in their play.

DISPLAY

Cover two tables with green cloth. Place a selection of woollen garments on one table. Add pictures of sheep and label the garments. On the other table, display the clay sheep with name labels made by the children.

WEEK 6
PETS

PERSONAL, SOCIAL AND EMOTIONAL DEVELOPMENT

- Use *The New Puppy* by Laurence Anholt (Orchard Books) to introduce the theme for the week. Talk about the reasons why Anna wanted a puppy and the things that the dog did to upset her. How would the group feel if their new puppy chewed their favourite slippers? (PS3, 4)

- Explain that at the end of the week there will be a pets event to which families and friends will be invited. Talk about the things that will have to be done to organise the day. (PS2, 3, 7, 8)

- Use *I Want a Cat* by Tony Ross as the focus for a circle time (see activity opposite). (PS3, 8)

COMMUNICATION, LANGUAGE AND LITERACY

- Invite children to bring in a photograph or object that is associated with a pet. Help children to make labels for them for a group display about caring for pets. (Children who do not have a pet could draw a picture of a pet they would like to have or borrow an object from a relation or friend.) (L17, 19)

- Help children to make posters to advertise the pet event. They could also make invitations. (L16, 17, 19)

MATHEMATICAL DEVELOPMENT

- Sing a group pet song to the tune of 'Ten green bottles', for example, 'Ten brown bunnies, sitting in a field, And if one brown bunny should hop, hop, hop away'. Encourage children to make up actions to the words and to anticipate the number of pets left each time one goes. (M2, 5, 6)

- Play the 'Collect a pet' game (see activity opposite). (M2)

KNOWLEDGE AND UNDERSTANDING OF THE WORLD

- Invite a parent to bring a pet to show to the group. Plan with the children the questions they might like to ask and the types of things they might like to know. If several parents are willing to speak, a visit could take place each day of pet week. (K2, 9)

- Discuss how we keep ourselves healthy when sharing our environment with pets. Talk about the need to wash hands and use different utensils for food. Make 'Wash your hands' posters. (K2, 9)

- Show the group a dog's identity tag with a telephone number and postal code. Explain that all dogs must wear them and encourage the group to think about times when they would be useful. Talk about times when children might get lost and what they should do. Ask children to pretend to be dog owners and help them to make labels for their dogs. (K2)

PHYSICAL DEVELOPMENT

- Make pathways on the floor using ropes or bean bags. Encourage children to move along the paths as pets. (PD2, 3)

- Repeat the pathways activity with pairs of children as a puppy and an owner. Explain that when taking a dog for a walk the owner must ensure that the dog waits to cross the road and does not run ahead. Encourage the children who are puppies to keep with their owners and to stop when they do. (PD2, 3)

CREATIVE DEVELOPMENT

- From fur fabric cut out a snake about 15cm long. Help children to stick eyes onto their snakes. If the snake is draped over an arm and then stroked from head to the end the snake starts to curl. Encourage children to name their pet snakes and to use them for imaginative play. (C4)

- Set up the role-play area as a pet shop. Include a range of soft toy pets; magnetic fish with nets and rods; boxes and baskets; a cash register; paper and pens for making signs and posters; and boxes labelled as pet foods. (C4)

- Make fish tanks from large boxes. Use paint and a variety of blue and green papers and scraps to create a watery scene. Add goldfish cut from shiny or marbled paper, shells and pebbles. Cover the front of the box with cellophane. (C1, 4)

ACTIVITY: 'I WANT A CAT' CIRCLE TIME

Learning opportunity: Participating in a circle time, listening to others and taking it in turn to speak.

Early Learning Goal: Personal, Social and Emotional Development. Children will be able to maintain attention, concentrate and sit quietly when appropriate. They will work as part of a group or class taking turns and sharing fairly.

Resources: Cat toy or ornament, *I Want a Cat* by Tony Ross (Red Fox).

Key vocabulary: Cat, pet, circle, listening eyes, vocabulary within the book.

Organisation: Whole group seated on the floor in a circle.

WHAT TO DO:

Help children to remember the routine for circle times including: only the person holding the cat may speak; if you do not wish to speak, pass the cat on; listening eyes are ones that look at the person who is speaking.

Show the group the cover of the *I Want a Cat* book. Point out the name of the author and encourage children to think about what the book might be about. Read the story, ensuring that everyone can see the pictures. Ask children to imagine that they are the child in the story and to think about why she wanted a cat. Pass the cat around the circle and invite children to complete the sentence 'I want a cat because.......'. At the end of the book the child has changed her mind and wants a dog instead. Ask children in turn to suggest other animals that she could have had. Discuss how the girl behaved in the book. Finish by playing a game enjoyed by the group such as 'Stand up if you are wearing............ and change places' to reinforce listening and co-operation.

ACTIVITY: COLLECT A PET GAME

Learning opportunity: Counting and playing collaboratively.

Early Learning Goal: Mathematical Development. Children will be able to count reliably up to ten everyday objects.

Resources: 'Collect a pet' board (see diagram); small toy animals; a large die with the numerals one to five and the word 'vet' on the remaining face.

Key vocabulary: Numbers one to five, vet, pet, names for pets.

Organisation: Small groups of up to four children.

WHAT TO DO:

Show children the game board. Invite the children to help you to place the pets at intervals along the track.

Show children the die and check that they can recognise the numbers. Help the children to read the word 'vet'. Talk about how a vet can help pets. Explain that they are going to play the 'Collect a pet' game. Give each child a counter. Encourage them to take it in turn to throw the die and move their counter the corresponding number of places along the track. If they land on a space with a pet they collect it. 'Vet' means 'have another go'. The game finishes when all the children have reached the end of the track. At the end of the game, encourage children to count how many pets they have collected and how many remain on the board.

Note: The board can be used in a variety of topics with the animals replaced by other objects that relate to the chosen theme.

DISPLAY

Cover a large noticeboard with brightly coloured backing paper. Mount and display a selection of the children's posters and invites. Place a table in front of the board, cover with a cloth and arrange collected objects belonging to pets alongside pet photographs. Place the children's fish tanks underneath the table with a box of non-fiction books about pets.

Toy animals sitting on board.

BRINGING IT ALL TOGETHER

THE PET EVENT

Before starting the Animals topic, ask if any parents might be willing to bring a safe pet to the event. Aim to have a variety of creatures. Check children's medical records for any allergies and during the topic notice whether there are any children who might be frightened by the presence of a particular animal. Check local authority guidelines for having animals in school.

PREPARATION

Explain to children that the purpose of the pet event is to learn more about animals and to show things that have been made over the topic to their families and friends. Tell children about the pets that might come to the event and ask which ones they would like to see. Talk about the way that they will need to behave when the animals are present and why. Encourage children to think about how it might feel to be a pet in a room full of children and adults.

With the children plan and practise a small presentation in which they can show something that has been made during the topic, recite rhymes, sing songs and join in an animal parade wearing the masks or finger puppets that they have made.

Make a group mobile to show children's favourite pets. Provide each child with a bone cut from stiff card. Encourage them to write their name on one side and to draw a picture of their favourite pet on the other. Hang it in a prominent position to welcome visitors to the pet event.

FOOD

A range of animal-shaped foods could be made for the event. Ideas include animal-shaped biscuits, sugar mice and snakes made from a variety of swiss rolls cut into pieces and arranged on long platters in repeating patterns.

ACTIVITIES

Start the event with the animal parade. Choose a piece of music with a good beat such as one of the songs from Walt Disney's *Jungle Book* video. Encourage children to move in time to the music and, when it stops, to sit quietly ready to listen and to watch the showing of pets. Encourage children to talk about the pets along with their parent or carer. Make time for questions. The number of pets to be shown will depend on the children's concentration and, also, whether pets have been shown earlier in the week. Follow this with the presentation by children, ensuring that items by individual children are balanced with ones by the whole group. Doing this reduces the urge to fidget! Involve all children in reciting rhymes, singing songs used during the project and explaining their favourite animal facts in a 'Did you know?' slot. Finish the presentation with a reminder about the need to wash hands after handling pets.

Following the presentation, encourage children to show their families and friends displays and activities from the animal project, to look at the visiting pets and, once hands have been washed, to enjoy the food prepared for the event.

PET ALTERNATIVE

As an alternative to focusing on pets the event could be to raise funds for an animal charity such as the RSPCA or for guide and/or listening dogs. If organised well enough in advance, an education officer from an animal charity may be willing to come to the group. Equally, a person who uses a listening or guide dog might come to talk about the way the dogs help them and how they are trained and cared for. At the end of the event a collection could be taken using collection boxes decorated by the children with animal pictures cut from wrapping paper.

> **Safety note:**
> There are some animals and birds that you should avoid having in the nursery. The Association for Science Education (Tel: 01707 267411) publishes a useful book, *Be Safe*, that gives all the dos and donts of keeping animals.
> Always make sure that children wash their hands after handling any animal and be aware that some children may be allergic to animal fur.

RESOURCES

Note: *All books were available from leading booksellers at the time of writing.*

RESOURCES TO COLLECT:

- Soft toy animals.
- Toy farm.
- Toy animals for a jungle.
- Large blow-up jungle animals.
- Music for animal movement such as *The Carnival of Animals* by Saint-Saens.
- Animal-shaped biscuit cutters.
- Toy cash register.
- Large-holed sieves.
- Large-eyed plastic needles.

EVERYDAY RESOURCES:

- Large and small boxes and clear plastic containers.
- Papers and cards of different weights, colours and textures, for example sugar, corrugated card, silver and shiny papers.
- Dry powder paints for mixing and mixed paints for covering large areas and printing.
- Different sized paint brushes from household brushes to thin brushes for delicate work and a variety of paint mixing containers.
- A variety of drawing and colouring pencils, crayons, pastels and so on.
- Additional decorative and finishing materials such as sequins, felt, foils, glitter, tinsel, shiny wool and threads, beads, pieces of textiles, parcel ribbon, bubble wrap.
- Table covers.
- Sponges.
- Split pins.
- Clay.

STORIES

Rumble in the Jungle by Giles Andreae (Orchard Books).

The New Puppy by Laurence Anholt (Orchard Books).

Dear Zoo by Rod Campbell (Puffin Books).

The Very Hungry Caterpillar by Eric Carle (Puffin Books).

Kum-Man-Gur The Rainbow Servant by James Cowan (Barefoot Books).

Hector Sylvester by A Durant and A Parker (Collins).

Picasso the Green Tree Frog by Amanda Graham (Era).

Crafty Chameleon by Mwenye Hadithi and Adrienne Kennaway (Hodder Children's Books).

Further Doings of Milly-Molly-Mandy by Joyce Lankester Brisley (Puffin).

Emma's Lamb by Kim Lewis (Walker Books).

Friska the Sheep that was too Small by Rob Lewis (Hodder Wayland).

Morag and the Lamb by Joan Lingard (Walker Books).

Just You and Me by Sam McBratney (Walker Books).

Peace at Last by Jill Murphy (Walker Books).

Who Am I? by Judith Nicholls (Ladybird).

Dream Time Aboriginal Stories by Oodgero (Lothrop, Lee & Shepard Books).

Dinner Time by Jan Pienkowski (Orchard Books).

I Want a Cat! by Tony Ross (Red Fox).

Can't You Sleep Little Bear? by Martin Waddell (Walker Books).

Let's Go Home Little Bear by Martin Waddell (Walker Books).

Over in the Grasslands by Anna Wilson and Alison Bartlett (Macmillan Children's Books).

I Don't Want to go to Bed! by Julie Sykes and Tim Warnes (Little Tiger Press, Magi Publications).

Little Tiger's Big Surprise! by Julie Sykes and Tim Warnes (Little Tiger Press, Magi Publications).

NON FICTION

Early years animal care worksheets and teacher's notes are available from Supplies Dept, RSPCA, Causeway, Horsham, West Sussex, RH12 1HG (posters also available in Welsh).

SONGS

Okki-tokki-unga Action Songs for Children chosen by Beatrice Harrop, Linda Friend and David Gadsby (A & C Black).

Apusskido Songs for Children chosen by Beatrice Harrop, Peggy Blakely and David Gadsby (A & C Black).

Three Singing Pigs: Making Music with Traditional Stories by Kaye Umansky (A & C Black).

POEMS

Larry Lion's Rumbling Rhymes by Giles Andreae and David Wojtowycz (Macmillan's Children's Books).

First Verses compiled by John Foster (Oxford University Press).

This Little Puffin by Elizabeth Matterson (Puffin).

Playtime Rhymes for the Very Young selected by Shona McKellar (Dorling Kindersley).

COLLECTING EVIDENCE OF CHILDREN'S LEARNING

Monitoring children's development is an important task. Keeping a record of children's achievements will help you to see progress and will draw attention to those who are having difficulties for some reason. If a child needs additional professional help, such as speech therapy, your records will provide valuable evidence.

Records should be the result of collaboration between group leaders, parents and carers. Parents should be made aware of your record keeping policies when their child joins your group. Show them the type of records you are keeping and make sure they understand that they have an opportunity to contribute. As a general rule, your records should form an open document. Any parent should have access to records relating to his or her child. Take regular opportunities to talk to parents about children's progress. If you have formal discussions regarding children about whom you have particular concerns, a dated record of the main points should be kept.

KEEPING IT MANAGEABLE

Records should be helpful in informing group leaders, adult helpers and parents and always be for the benefit of the child. However, keeping records of every aspect of each child's development can become a difficult task. The sample shown will help to keep records manageable and useful. The golden rule is to keep them simple.

Observations will basically fall into three categories:

- **Spontaneous records:** Sometimes you will want to make a note of observations as they happen, for example when a child is heard counting cars accurately during a play activity, or is seen to play collaboratively for the first time.

- **Planned observations:** Sometimes you will plan to make observations of children's developing skills in their everyday activities. Using the learning opportunity identified for an activity will help you to make appropriate judgements about children's capabilities and to record them systematically.

To collect information:

- talk to children about their activities and listen to their responses;

- listen to children talking to each other;

- observe children's work such as early writing, drawings, paintings and 3-d models. (Keeping photocopies or photographs is sometimes useful.)

Sometimes you may wish to set up 'one-off' activities for the purposes of monitoring development. Some groups, for example, ask children to make a drawing of themselves at the beginning of each term to record their progressing skills in both co-ordination and observation. Do not attempt to make records following every activity!

- **Reflective observations:** It is useful to spend regular time reflecting on the progress of a few children (about four children each week). Aim to make some brief comments about each child every half term.

INFORMING YOUR PLANNING

Collecting evidence about children's progress is time-consuming but essential. When you are planning, use the information you have collected to help you to decide what learning opportunities you need to provide next for children. For example, a child who has poor pencil or brush control will benefit from more play with dough or construction toys to build the strength of hand muscles.

Example of recording chart

Name: Paul Green		D.O.B. 17.5.96		Date of entry: 13.9.98	
Term	**Personal, Social and Emotional Development**	**Communication, Language and Literacy**	**Mathematical Development**	**Knowledge and Understanding of the World**	**Physical Development**	**Creative Development**
ONE	Reluctant to say good bye to mother. Prefers adult company 20.9.00 EMH	Enjoys listening to stories. Particularly liked *Friska*. Can write first name. Good pencil grip 20.10.00 EMH	Is able to say numbers to ten and count accurately five objects. Short concentration when playing games with a die. 5.11.00 EHL	Very eager to ask questions. Is fascinated by all facts about wild animals. 16.10.00 LSS	Can balance on one leg. Loved being an animal and walking like an elephant. Does not like the feel of playdough. 16.10.00 SJS	Made a wonderful camouflage collage. Enjoys painting particularly when mixing own colours. 16.10.00 EHL
TWO						
THREE						

SKILLS OVERVIEW OF SIX-WEEK PLAN

Week	Topic focus	Personal, Social and Emotional Development	Communication, Language and Literacy	Mathematical Development	Knowledge and Understanding of the World	Physical Development	Creative Development
1	Name the animals	Listening; Expressing emotions; Sensitivity to others needs	Listening to stories Role play; Recognising initial sounds	Counting Using comparative language	Comparing Talking Describing	Moving with control, safety, awareness of space and imagination; Using malleable materials	Printing Making sounds
2	Where I live	Listening; Expressing emotions	Listening to stories and rhymes; Listening; Writing; Recognising initial sounds	Counting Using language of addition and subtraction	Observing Comparing; Describing Talking	Moving with control, safety, awareness of space and imagination; Using large equipment	Collage Painting Using materials
3	Hide and seek	Listening Considering actions Expressing emotions	Listening to stories Speaking Writing	Counting Recognising numbers	Talking; Observing Comparing; Describing Constructing	Moving with control, safety, awareness of space and imagination	Drawing Painting; Collage Weaving
4	Young animals	Sensitivity to others Speaking Listening	Listening to stories Responding to stories Retelling stories	Comparative language; Counting Recognising numbers	Talking Constructing	Moving with control safety, awareness of space and imagination	Printing; Collage Painting Using materials
5	Farm animals	Taking turns Listening Speaking	Writing for a purpose Recognising initial sounds; Discussing	Counting; Recognising numbers; Using comparative language	Talking Comparing Constructing	Moving with control, safety, awareness of space and imagination; Using malleable materials	Using materials Playing percussion Sewing
6	Pets	Speaking; Listening Collaborative planning	Reciting rhymes Writing for a purpose	Counting; Using language of addition and subtraction	Talking Observing Describing	Moving with control, safety, imagination, and awareness of space	Using materials Role play

HOME LINKS

The theme of Animals lends itself to useful links with children's homes and families. Through working together children and adults gain respect for each other and build comfortable and confident relationships.

ESTABLISHING PARTNERSHIPS

- Keep parents informed about the topic of Animals, the themes for each week and the proposed date for the pet event. By understanding the work of the group, parents will enjoy the involvement of contributing ideas, time and resources.

- Photocopy the parent's page for each child to take home.

- Invite friends, childminders and families to join in the pet event.

- Invite a parent to record the pet event with photographs for a group big book.

VISITING ENTHUSIASTS

- Invite adults to come to the group to show safe pets. Ask them to talk about what it means to have pets and how they take responsibility for them.

- Contact the education officer for a local or national animal charity, farm or sanctuary. Many will visit to give talks to children and may be able to provide a range of resources.

RESOURCE REQUESTS

- Ask parents to contribute toys on the animal theme.

- Make a collection of animal posters and photographs.

- Scraps of fabric, wool and wrapping paper are invaluable for collage work and a wide range of interesting activities.

THE PET EVENT

- It is always useful to have extra adults at times such as the event.

- Invite parents to contribute animal-shaped refreshments that have been made with children at home.